FEATS of 21st-CENTURY ENGINEERING

21st-CENTURY CARS

Published in 2019 by Enslow Publishing, LLC.
101 W. 23rd Street, Suite 240, New York, NY 10011

Copyright © 2019 by Enslow Publishing, LLC.

Library of Congress Cataloging-in-Publication Data

Names: Niver, Heather Moore, author.
Title: 21st century cars / Heather Moore Niver.
Description: New York : Enslow Publishing, 2019. |
Series: Feats of 21st century engineering | Includes bibliographical references
and index. | Audience: Grades 3–6. |
Identifiers: LCCN 2017050821| ISBN 9780766096974 (library bound) |
ISBN 978 0766096981 (pbk.)
Subjects: LCSH: Automobiles–Technological innovations–Juvenile literature.
Classification: LCC TL147 .N56 2019 | DDC 629.222–dc23
LC record available at https://lccn.loc.gov/2017050821

Printed in the United States of America

To Our Readers: We have done our best to make sure all website addresses in this
book were active and appropriate when we went to press. However, the author
and the publisher have no control over and assume no liability for the material
available on those websites or on any websites they may link to. Any comments or
suggestions can be sent by e-mail to customerservice@enslow.com.

Photo Credits: Cover, p. 1 (technical drawing) pluie_r/Shutterstock.com; cover,
p. 1 (sports car) Michal Bednarek/Shutterstock.com; p. 4 Kobby Dagan/Shutterstock
.com; pp. 6-7 Deniz Toprak/Shutterstock.com; p. 9 Paul Fearn/Alamy Stock
Photo; p. 11 Stock Montage/Archive Photos/Getty Images; p. 13 Science &
Society Picture Library/Getty Images; p. 15 Hulton Archive/Getty Images;
p. 18 Allan Tannenbaum/The LIFE Images Collection/Getty Images; pp. 20-21
Michael Gottschalk/Photothek/Getty Images; pp. 22-23 Bettmann/Getty Images;
pp. 24-25, 36-37 VanderWolf Images/Shutterstock.com; p. 28 Roslan Rahman/
AFP/Getty Images; p. 30 AFP/Getty Images; pp. 32-33 Bloomberg/Getty Images;
p. 38 PaulLP/Shutterstock.com; p. 39 Yamada Hitoshi/ABACAUSA.COM/Newscom;
p. 41 Barcroft Media/Getty Images.

CONTENTS

Cars of the twenty-first century will be smarter, faster, more innovative, and better for the environment. This Eli Electric car was displayed at a 2017 auto show.

Introduction

Engineers are among the most forward-looking people in the world. They are always trying to solve problems, refine performance, and improve safety. Engineers in the automotive industry do some of the most exciting, cutting-edge work. And they have some of the most ingenious inventions. Think the idea of the flying car seems a little bizarre? Engineers think, "A flying car could help solve the problem of traffic jams on the world's most congested highways." Maybe a flying car used to seem more like science fiction, but engineers are working on designs for some possibilities right now!

Human beings have been working on ways to move around more efficiently throughout history. The invention of the automobile mobilized people more than ever. Engineers are always looking for ways to make cars faster, safer, and more efficient. They also want to solve a whole lot of other issues that have come about as cars have changed over the years.

Famous artist and inventor Leonardo da Vinci may have engineered the first automobiles, at least on paper. Leonardo is well known for his inventive sketches, but as far back as the early 1500s he saw a problem and knew it needed to be solved. People needed to move from here to there quickly. Leonardo drew a sketch of a mechanical cart that was not pulled by horses. This was revolutionary!

At the 2017 Istanbul auto show, this Bugatti Veyron EB Grand Sport shows off just one example of the exciting ideas and innovations modern engineers have been dreaming up.

Unfortunately, Leonardo did not see his clever design become a realization. But his sketch shows that the desire for faster, more efficient transportation goes back a long way. And he wasn't the only one eager to be on the move.

In 1600, the Chinese were sailing around in chariots propelled by the wind. And around the same time, in Holland, Simon Steven built something similar. It could hold twenty-eight people and travel 39 miles (62 kilometers) in about two hours.

Automobiles in the twenty-first century are certainly worlds away from what Leonardo da Vinci or the Chinese were dreaming up. Just as engineers have always done through the years, today's inventors are still dreaming, scheming, and solving new problems in the automobile industry. Concept cars show off the newest and most fantastic ideas in technology, safety features, and more. New materials, techniques, and style ideas are always flowing. Keep reading to learn some of the highlights of the history of automotive engineering and some fun and exciting features like safety, style, and speed!

1

The Development of the Car

Cars have changed dramatically since the first model debuted. That first model was more of a "horseless carriage" than today's accomplishments of engineering. But compared to the simple horse and carriage, each improvement and technological advance was a feat in and of itself.

Carriages

Before anything resembling the car as we now know it came to be, there was the carriage. At first, inventors simply adapted horse carts to work with engines, so of course the early models were called "horseless carriages." In 1769, Nicolas Cugnot developed a three-wheeled carriage for moving pieces of artillery, or weapons. It rolled around on three wheels and was powered by steam. But it could run for only twenty minutes at 2.25 miles (3.6 km) per hour! Then it needed to stop to build up a fresh supply of steam. Cugnot's carriage offered transportation for four. This was probably the rollout of the first automotive vehicle.

Steam carriages continued to be developed in the eighteenth and nineteenth centuries, including one in the United States in 1805

Oliver Evans developed a unique and marvelous vehicle in 1805. His steam carriage ran not only on land but also on water.

by Oliver Evans. The US development was a combination vehicle that ran on land and water! It looked a lot like a tractor and carried ten people. From there, the route to creating the modern car continued to be as varied and intriguing as these roots.

Send in the Steam

As the 1900s drew near, almost one hundred manufacturers were cranking out steam automobiles. In 1897, twin brothers from America, Francis E. and Freelan O. Stanley, offered up the Stanley Steamer.

Kerosene-heated water created steam in the car's tank, and the pressure from the steam triggered the driving machinery. It was a simple way to power the car, but it had a few drawbacks. First, it took a long time to heat the water enough to propel the car. Second, rumors swirled that this method might make the car explode, although research proved this wasn't true. The Stanley brothers proved determined and built more than two hundred models, called the Stanley Runabout, between 1898 and 1899. The popularity of this car lost steam around World War I (1914–1918) and stopped production in 1929.

The Auto Electric

The next feat in automotive technology was an electric car, powered by battery. A few were developed in Europe during the 1880s. In 1891, William Morrison began producing the first electric cars in the United States. More than fifty other manufacturers started to produce them, too. They put out about thirty-five thousand electric cars between 1896 and 1915. Some of the most popular "electrics," as they were known, were named the Columbia, the Baker, and the Riker.

Among the benefits of the electric car was its smooth ride and easy operation. Unfortunately, it didn't run well at speeds above 20 miles (32 km) per hour. It also needed to have its batteries recharged after about every 50 miles (80 km). Electric cars of this time were only practical for driving distances, like in cities.

On the Go with Gasoline

In the 1860s, a Belgian inventor named Étienne Lenoir changed the future of cars. When he was just twelve years old, he knew what he wanted to do. He said, "When I grow up, I'll make machinery, new machinery, machinery walking all alone." He went on to do just that. Lenoir designed and built a gas engine that ran on a combination

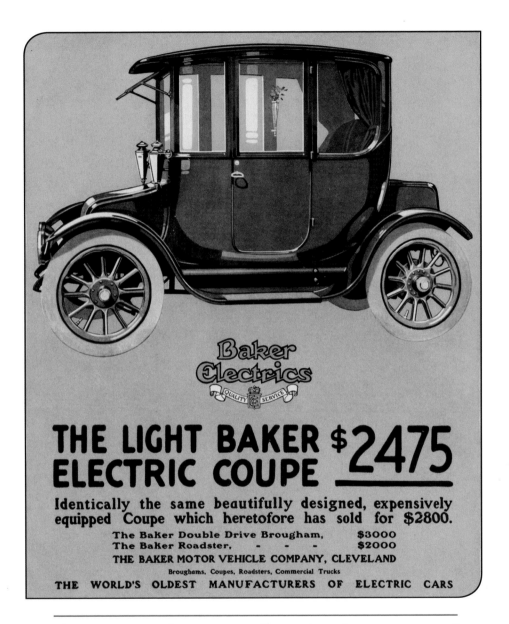

Baker Electrics
QUALITY SERVICE

THE LIGHT BAKER ELECTRIC COUPE $2475

Identically the same beautifully designed, expensively equipped Coupe which heretofore has sold for $2800.

The Baker Double Drive Brougham, $3000
The Baker Roadster,   -   -   - $2000

THE BAKER MOTOR VEHICLE COMPANY, CLEVELAND

Broughams, Coupes, Roadsters, Commercial Trucks

THE WORLD'S OLDEST MANUFACTURERS OF ELECTRIC CARS

This magazine advertisement from 1915 showcases one of the most popular "electrics" that were all the rage, called the Light Baker Electric Coupe automobile.

of coal gas and air. Some of these machines were built so well that they were still humming along perfectly even after twenty years of constant use! By 1865, more than 1,400 gas engines were running in France and Britain. They were used for jobs that did not require much power, like printing and pumping.

In 1862, Lenoir built an entire vehicle that could run on that engine. He changed his engine so that it was powered by liquid fuel. His vehicle was able to successfully complete a trip of 6 miles (10 km) over two or three hours. Eventually, he made the engine even more efficient and connected it to a wagon with three wheels. Some stories say that his vehicle made a historic trip of 50 miles (80 km), but there are debates over whether it happened or if it is just an exaggeration.

Siegfried Marcus of Austria built several four-wheeled gasoline-powered vehicles. Some controversy swirls around his inventions, notably his design of a vehicle that cruised along at 10 miles (16 km) per hour. If he actually made it, it would have been the direct relation to our modern autos as the first to be powered by gasoline and an engine with four cylinders. But no solid evidence exists to prove that he built it as early as 1875. Rather, evidence points to a later date of 1888–1889.

In 1876, German engineer Nikolaus Otto invented the first successful internal combustion gasoline engine. Otto and his brother had learned about Lenoir's gas engine in 1860. Inspired, they tried building their own version. Despite their enthusiasm, the engine puttered out after a couple of minutes. His brother was discouraged and walked away from the project, but Otto continued on with it. Otto found a willing partner in Eugen Langen. Langen was a technician and owned a sugar factory. Otto quit his job as a salesman of tea, coffee, and sugar, and the two men started the very first engine manufacturing company, Otto & Cie. Today the company is known as DEUTZ AG, Köln.

Nikolaus Otto, together with Eugen Langen, pioneered the four-stroke internal combustion engine in 1876.

Behold, Bertha Benz

Karl Benz's wife, Bertha, wanted to show that the Motor Car was useful. So she took it on its first long-distance drive— without telling her husband! In August 1888, she and their two oldest sons drove 66 miles (106 km) over two days. They solved some problems on their drive. Bertha used a hatpin to clear out the fuel pipe when it clogged. She used her garter, a band used to hold up a stocking, to insulate a wire.

Bertha Benz's journey caught the attention of the press. Some still looked skeptically on what they called the "smoking monster," but others were eager to try it.

At the 1867 Paris World Exhibition, Otto & Cie won a gold medal for a gas engine they built that year. That engine is called a four-stroke compressed charge engine. This engine, also known as an internal combustion engine, uses the power created when fuel burns and explodes to push a piston located inside a cylinder. It is known as the Otto cycle engine, and the term "Otto cycle" now refers to all compressed charge, four-cycle engines.

By 1885, the public was able to buy gasoline-fueled automobiles. Karl Benz of Mannheim, Germany, offered the Motorwagen, which had three wheels and reached speeds of 6 miles (10 km) per hour (about the same as a brisk walking pace). On January 29, 1886, Benz got a patent for his Motor Car. But to his dismay, nobody seemed interested in buying it. Benz became known for being on the cutting edge of autos for the time, especially for his innovative combination design of the internal combustion engine with a chassis.

Gottlieb Daimler

German Gottlieb Daimler was also on the forefront of automobile history. He studied engineering in school and worked for a number of engineering companies, gaining more and more experience with engines. One handy connection came in 1872 when he worked for Deutz Gasmotorenfabrik. This company was part-owned by none other than Nikolaus Otto. Daimler and Wilhelm Maybach left Otto's company and started building engines on their own.

In 1885, Daimler and his design partner Maybach improved on Otto's internal combustion engine, creating what is now widely considered the model for the gas engine so prevalent today. This new engine was revolutionary for its small, light design, as well as for its efficiency. On March 8, 1886, Daimler adapted a stagecoach in which to hold the engine, a four-wheeled automobile. He had invented the first useful internal combustion engine.

Gottlieb Daimler and Wilhelm Maybach joined forces to create engines on their own, eventually resulting in vehicles such as this 1894 convertible car.

Daimler didn't stop there. Besides improving his engine, in 1889 he and Maybach did something new. Instead of fitting an engine into an existing vehicle, they built their entire structure. This automobile boasted a four-speed transmission and could motor along at speeds up to 10 miles (16 km) per hour. The next year, Daimler established Daimler Motoren-Gesellschaft, where he could build his creations. Maybach went on to create the Mercedes in 1901.

The Industry Takes Off

The early 1900s effectively marked the beginning of the automobile industry. In the United States, a number of inventors were hard at work on new models. American brothers J. Frank and Charles E. Duryea had successfully created a gasoline-powered automobile in 1893. In 1896, they began commercially producing their Duryea car. That very same year, in Detroit, Michigan, Henry Ford was puttering down the streets in his horseless carriage, terrifying the horses! In New York City, the first automobile salesroom flung open its doors to the public, thanks to Percy Owen, and the first auto show was held.

Ransom E. Olds saw that the popular car needed to be produced faster and in larger numbers. He had been tinkering with various experiments for five years before he began mass production of autos at Olds Motor Works in 1901. His Oldsmobile sold for $650. Meanwhile Ford and Henry M. Leland started improving their mass production techniques in the early 1900s. Ford installed the first conveyor belt assembly line around 1913–1914, which significantly reduced the time it took to assemble an automobile.

Pollution Reducers and Fuel Efficiency

T hroughout the twentieth century, cars became more comfortable and easier to operate. Manufacturers developed power steering and brakes. They gave the vehicles more controls over things like windows and seat position.

But as more people relied on cars, fuel supply became a problem. The United States no longer had enough gasoline, which comes from oil. With its own oil supplies dangerously low, the US government had to reach out to other countries. In 1973, many of the world's oil-producing countries no longer shipped this precious commodity to the countries that needed it. Besides spiking prices, automobile makers realized that they needed to find other ways to fuel their cars, or at least to fuel them more efficiently.

Pollution Problem

It also came to light that as gasoline burned, it sent poisonous gases into the air. Cars were causing a lot of air pollution. Big changes had to be made. One answer was to change the gasoline engines. Making engines that perform more efficiently and giving them emission-

In 1973, fuel became so scarce that cars lined up at the pumps to make sure they could fill their tanks when it was available.

control devices definitely helped. But engineers wanted to invent cars that were even better.

In 1975, engineers made a huge development in automobile emissions. Catalytic converters were added to cars. Catalytic converters are added to a car's exhaust system. They convert, or change, the gas from a harmful one into a safer gas before it leaves the car.

(Re)Enter Electric

Electric vehicles (or EVs as they are now called) became a technology of interest again after the 1970s gas crisis. But these storage battery–powered autos were expensive and had some technological problems. By 1990, the General Electric Company announced the Impact, an experimental car that promised to run as smoothly as an internal combustion engine car. It was discontinued, though, because it was so expensive to produce.

The Charging Challenge

Electric cars have become more common, for passengers and even for mail delivery. But they still have some problems that need to be solved before more people buy them. For example, electric cars need to be charged every so often. Engineers are working to invent cars that hold longer charges all the time. But in the meantime, some major US highways are offering charging stations.

By 2017, engineers had developed two types of charging stations. Single-phase and three-phase AC charging stations are most common. They are not too tough or expensive to install. But the drawback is the time it takes to charge a car. No one wants to have to spend hours in the middle of a trip waiting for his or her car to recharge. High-speed DC chargers, however, are rather expensive to install. Although they charge cars quickly, few of them can be found out on the road. Furthermore, not all cars are set up to use DC charging.

Plug It In

As the charging time for electric cars becomes even faster and cars become more efficient, another problem arises. Current EV owners want to make sure the plug design, hardware, and software will be compatible with the newest options for charging. The concept known as AllCharge by Continental might ease the minds of worried EV

Because some cars run on batteries that need to be recharged, many highways provide charging stations.

drivers. AllCharge allows the car to be charged any number of ways, including at almost any charging station. A single cable connects the car to the charger, whatever it may be, and converts the power as needed. In some cases, just five minutes of charging can get a car another 93 miles (150 km) down the highway. AllCharge offers an added bonus, too. It can also be a source of power for electric devices like laptop computers or microwaves.

Currently, the car that boasts the most distance on one charge is 2017 Tesla Model 3, at 310 miles (499 km). But knowing engineers, they are already working on boosting that.

India states that it hopes to sell only electric cars by 2030. Faced with terrible air pollution that causes as many as 1.2 million deaths a year, India is also one of the top three oil importers. Besides being better for the environment, this move could save the country $60 billion. Now that will be a feat!

Car companies are following suit, too. Volvo wants to sell only electric or hybrid cars as soon as 2019. It's possible that gasoline-powered cars will soon be a thing of the past.

Do We Diesel?

A handful of passenger cars run on a different type of fuel called diesel. Diesel fuel is less expensive than gasoline and boasts between 20 and 30 percent more miles or kilometers per gallon. But diesel isn't the answer, either. First and foremost, it causes tremendous pollution. And diesel vehicles tend to be much noisier, causing noise pollution. Still, engineers have not stopped trying to figure out how to make diesel a more useful fuel.

Alternative Energy

Some automakers have developed vehicles that run on alternative energy such as biofuel, like ethanol, or batteries. Other materials can be used to make fuel, too. These include coal, oil, shale, or tar sands.

Ethanol

Ethyl alcohol, better known as ethanol, is used alone or at other times is mixed with gasoline to make gasohol. This renewable resource is made from plant sources like corn and sugarcane. It is easy to make. Most vehicles can be easily adapted to use it. Countries like Brazil use ethanol, as they have a substantial sugar crop. In the Philippines, some cars run on an ethanol that is made from condensed coconut husks.

But engineers have found that ethanol isn't the perfect fuel, either. In most countries, manufacturing it is expensive. Ethanol can also damage metal engine parts when they come in contact with high concentrations of the fuel. Continuing research might mean that ethanol could eventually be used more commonly.

Methanol

Methanol is another gas alternative. Also known as methyl alcohol or wood alcohol, methanol is extracted from wood products or natural gas, which is presently the most efficient way of getting it. It can also be distilled from food waste, garbage, and other organic sources. Methanol was fairly popular in the 1990s, but the price of natural gas spiked. It became too expensive to make methanol. And car manufacturers in the United States stopped making cars that could use it.

Ethanol, which is made from corn and sugarcane, is a renewable resource that is sometimes mixed with gasoline to make gasohol.

Methanol has several positive features that made it a good use for fuel. It is inexpensive to produce, compared to other non-gasoline fuels. It is also safer to use because it is not as flammable as gasoline. And because it can be made from natural gas and feedstock, the United States could make it and reduce the need to import fuel from other countries. Natural gas is easier to come by through a process called fracking, which has a number of environmental issues. Fracking causes a lot of wastewater, for example, which pollutes areas near where it occurs. There is also some concern that fracking causes earthquakes.

Methanol is used in the car racing industry because it creates more power and works well for boosting engines. It takes more methanol to run a car, though, making it less efficient. And if it is left in a vehicle, it can corrode fuel lines.

Hello, Hybrid

Hybrids seem like a modern invention, but one hybrid called the Lohner-Porsche Elektromobil was shown in Paris back in 1900. It used a battery-powered motor developed by Ferdinand Porsche in a coach made by Jacob Lohner. The Elektromobil was electric, but soon they added an internal combustion engine to keep the battery charged.

Hybrids use some gasoline and some electricity. Hybrid vehicles combine an extremely efficient gas or diesel engine with a battery system or electric motor. The engines are very light yet put out a whole lot of power. The car is always working at its most efficient level, based on the kind of driving the operator is doing. Advanced electronics in the engine and transmission controls make this happen.

Showcased in 2015, this Toyota Prius hybrid always runs at maximum efficiency using a combination of gasoline and electricity to speed down the highway.

As the car is driving, it becomes its own battery charger and recharges the battery. This is a clear bonus because there isn't a need to find an electrical outlet to plug the car into when the charge gets low. Smaller engines and cars that work more efficiently are clearly a major feat of engineering. But these vehicles are very complicated to manufacture, and so they are expensive to buy.

Another answer to the gasoline issue is the plug-in hybrid or plug-in hybrid-electric vehicle (PHEV). These hybrids have special batteries that can be plugged into an electrical outlet or charging station. These batteries then store electricity, which means the car uses less fuel when driving.

Safe and Sound

The earliest cars were likely exciting to ride in—but dangerous! Safety has become a primary concern for automobile manufacturers. Seat belts and airbags help keep everyone in the car as safe as possible in case of a crash. The newest cars perform better in a crash so that passenger injuries are minimized and the car is less likely to be totaled, or wrecked beyond repair.

Hands Off the Wheel

Some cars have been engineered to drive without much, or any, help from a driver. Many cars have had semiautonomous features since the 1990s. This means the cars stop, steer, and accelerate with little help from the driver. Some Teslas have autopilot features that do this. A human still drives the car, but this feature keeps the car in the lane and pays attention to surrounding cars using sensors. Some cars have "driver assist features." They have lane assist, adaptive cruise control, and self-braking systems. BMW, Infiniti, and Mercedes-Benz have all released semiautonomous cars. In the Mercedes-Benz, for example, all a driver needs to do to change lanes is hit the turn signal for two seconds and the car takes it from there.

**A self-driving, or autonomous, car cruises down the street
in Southeast Asia during a test run with a safety driver.**

Fully autonomous cars are an engineering feat that is not far off. Google, Tesla, and Apple are all in a heated competition to come out with completely autonomous cars. Samsung and Hyundai have tested autonomous cars in Korea.

In 2017, Audi announced its A8, which will accelerate, brake, and steer on its own. But this can only occur on divided highways during traffic jams when the car is going less than 37 miles (60 km) per hour. And it will not change lanes. A camera features safety mechanisms, such as watching to make sure the driver is ready to take over within ten seconds so that the driver cannot kick back and read a book during a drive. It even has a couple of bonus options, such as foot massagers in the back seat! Known as Traffic Jam Pilot, Audi has no plans to offer it in the United States and some other countries until some legal issues are figured out.

Tesla offers a feature called Autopilot, which allows the car to make its way through traffic using a camera, radar on the bumper, and special sensors on the front and rear. Similarly, Traffic Jam Assist from Bosch helps guide drivers through traffic, whether it's heavy or an outright jam. The car can simply drive off and automatically accelerate and brake. Sometimes it can also steer. This technology uses cameras and radar.

Google's Waymo program might offer the most advanced autonomous vehicle technology, according to some. In Phoenix, Arizona, Google is offering Early Rider, free test drives in Lexus SUVs and Chrysler Pacifica minivans. Many people are not convinced that self-driving cars are safe, so Waymo vehicles give them the chance to try it out with a test driver on hand to ensure safety. In Pittsburgh, Pennsylvania, some lucky passengers received self-driving rides in 2016 from ride-sharing company Uber. Boston company nuTonomy made a similar offer available in Singapore.

A Kangaroo Challenge

But autonomous cars have run into problems. For example, in Australia, Volvo's self-driving cars are baffled by the way kangaroos hop! These cars have a feature called the Large Animal Detection system. Large beasts such as moose and elk have not been a problem, but the unpredictable hopping of the kangaroo proves to be too much. Volvo is continuing to work on technologies that will not be so confused by this bouncing beast.

In 2016, the ride-sharing service Uber offered passengers in Pittsburgh, Pennsylvania, the opportunity to take a spin in their autonomous vehicles.

Stop!

City driving can be stressful. Stop-and-go traffic requires a lot of braking and accelerating, switching from the gas pedal to the brake, and a clutch for manual cars. Engineers have introduced a possible solution for that. Rather than a traditional brake pedal, they have regenerative braking technology. With a single pedal for acceleration

Work Commute Workouts?

Some engineers are thinking about how drivers in autonomous vehicles can put their spare time to good use. How about a gym on wheels? Bus carpools can carry a group of people who work out on the way to work. Because autonomous vehicles are considered so much safer (statistics show that 94 percent of crashes are thanks to human error), there is less need to be buckled into a seat. Autonomous coffee shop buses already exist, so the possibility of a gym on the go isn't all that bizarre an idea.

and deceleration, the driver takes their foot off the pedal completely to stop. BMW i3, Volkswagen Golf, Chevrolet Bolt EV, and the 2018 Nissan Leaf all use this technology. In the Leaf, there is a simple switch: "With the flip of a switch, the technology turns your accelerator into an e-Pedal, allowing drivers to accelerate, decelerate and stop using just the e-Pedal. e-Pedal technology is the world's first one-pedal operation that allows drivers to bring the car to a complete stop even on hills, stay in position, and resume driving instantly." For now there is still a brake pedal in the Leaf. Nissan claims its e-Pedal is simpler than that of the other models.

Car Talk

Another 2017 safety feature might sound a little like science fiction, but vehicle-to-vehicle communication (V2V) is real. It is available in the Mercedes-Benz E-Class car. Yes, cars can talk to each other. They use radio signals to share traffic warnings to others in the area, like when someone runs a red light up the road just seconds after it is detected. It only works within the Benz cars, but it does increase safety.

Future Features

While handy safety features like Traffic Jam Assist sense the surrounding environment, Ford is experimenting with LiDAR (Light Detection And Ranging) systems. With this technology, cars "see" the surrounding environment as it happens, in real time.

Inside the car, biometrics could pay attention to the driver. If he or she falls asleep at the wheel, sensors note it and the car takes over. The car might pull off the road and turn off, for example. Others might sense if the driver is showing signs of nodding off and trigger a warning to alert them. It can monitor breathing and heart rate, too, and take control if the driver passes out or has a heart attack. Some engineering might help the car sense when an accident might happen and adjust things in the car for safety, like closing windows or moving the steering wheel and seats.

Engineers are also working on options that focus on comfort. Some car companies like Audi are working on engineering a personal intelligent assistant. With this

A potential customer (*left*) checks out Nissan Motor Co.'s e-Pedal technology, a single-pedal that speeds up, slows down, and stops their Leaf electric vehicle (EV).

feature, if the driver has an appointment on her smartphone, the car will automatically put the location of the appointment on a control screen. Just tap the screen and you're on your way! If a contact is associated with the appointment, their information will pop up so the driver can text or call them. Gas tank low? The assistant suggests the driver stop and fuel up.

Feeling stressed? Future Audi cars might help ease that on the way home. Time in the car can be used for relaxing breathing exercises and a massaging seat that even matches the rhythm of the music.

The Need for Speed

Fast, fun cars benefit from the most daring engineering of all. Race cars and sports cars have been speeding faster and faster ever since the first rubber hit the road.

Many sports cars and race cars perform better than ever thanks to high-tech materials. Graphene, for example, is a kind of carbon that is considered a "wonder material" for its thinness and strength (it is two hundred times stronger than steel). Aerogel is another material making its way into the newest autos. It was first used to insulate NASA's space suits. And gorilla glass is as mighty as it sounds. This glass is hardened by chemicals and weighs around half as much as regular laminated glass. Gorilla glass is used in many smartphones, too. Another alternative to carbon fiber is nanocellulose. It is less expensive, and its use could cut down on a car's weight as well as help it use fuel more effectively.

Cool Concepts: Concept Cars

Some of the most exciting cars are concept cars, which are made to show off new ideas and technology.

Porsche is known for is sports cars and race cars, but in recent years it has diversified. Porsche has presented an electric model concept car, the Cayman. This speedy sports car has a super-fast charging system called Porsche Turbo Charging. It is advertised as making average charging connections even faster. The electric Cayman can zip from 0 to 60 miles (0–97 km) per hour in 3.3 seconds and race along for about 124 miles (200 km). A more modest car, the Mission E, is due in 2020. This model can go for more than 310 miles (499 km) after charging for just fifteen minutes.

The sports car maker Porsche has expanded from race cars into the area of electric cars with its Mission E electronic sports car, due in 2020.

Jaguar was not really in the "green" car race. It did present the concept plug-in hybrid called the C-X75 but never took the concept any further. That is, until 2019's I-Pace Concept electric vehicle. Its battery offers 220 miles (354 km) on just one charge, and it can reach that good-old 60 miles (97 km) per hour in only four seconds.

Super Stingray Corvette

Many car enthusiasts love a fast car, and Chevrolet's Corvette is at the top of many lists, with models for highway and for racing around the track. The C7, known as the Stingray, was a convertible released in 2017. For those with a need for speed, the Stingray can help make the driving experience even better. *Consumer Reports*' review described it as having "ferocious acceleration, precise handling, and excellent braking." The review also mentioned a few other perks, such as the car's "thrilling" acceleration, high levels of handling grip, and fantastic looks. It also has eight speeds, compared to the six offered in the 2015 model. A Performance Data Recorder can record video of a driving session and offer real-time data during the drive. It can all be saved to a memory card to review later and learn how to improve the driving.

Other C7 models have headed to the racetrack and won numerous times, but Chevy engineers are still working on improvements. One major change in the next car, a C8, is the location of the engine. This new racer may be a Corvette with a mid-engine. In a mid-engine auto, power is located behind the driver instead of in front. Ferrari's 488 GTE and the Ford GT already made this switch in 2016 and gave the C7 a run

The Corvette C7, also known as a Stingray, sizzles on the highway as it accelerates to heart-racing speeds. Rather than the previous six speeds, the Stingray features eight.

for its money on the track. The C7 held its ground, but engineers took note of the challenge from the other mid-engine cars.

Excellently Fast Electric Cars

Just because a car is electric doesn't mean it can't be fast. Some engineers realized that drivers wanted an electric car and speed. And why not? The Tesla Model S has an option called "Ludicrous Mode" that gives the driver enough power to speed from 0 to 60 miles (0–97 km) per hour in a blink of an eye: 2.8 seconds! (A previous model had an "Insane Mode.")

Always improving and modifying, Tesla is at work on a 2019 model for its Roadster Sport. The older Roadster Sport electric vehicle (EV) could motor along for about 200 miles (320 km) on a single charge and zip from 0 to 60 (0–97 km) per hour in 3.7 seconds. Its top speed

This 2012 model Tesla Roadster Sport is an electric vehicle that could cruise for 200 miles (320 km) on just one charge. Future versions are sure to improve on it.

was 125 mph (201 kph). The newest EV will have the fastest 0 to 60 so far.

There's also Genovation eXtreme Electric (GXE), which is a 2006 Chevrolet Corvette Z06 that was adapted by Genovation. The GXE has been clocked at 186.8 miles (300.6 km) per hour. It has a light body and can zip along for 130 miles (209 km) before it needs to stop and recharge.

Plenty of other EVs are being built for speed, too. Shelby SuperCars (SSC North America) created the Aero EV (2006–2013) that could zoom from 0 to 60 miles (0–97 km) in just 2.5 seconds. It could reach speeds of more than 200 miles (320 km), too. And all this speed can happen after just ten minutes of fast charging.

BMW has also put a car in the EV race with its i3. Although it is meant for city driving, the i3 can race up to 100 miles (161 km) per hour and do the whole 0 to 60 miles (0–97 km) per hour thing in 7.2 seconds.

And to keep the speedy, green ideas fresh and flowing, there is the EcoCAR Advanced Vehicle Technology Competition. The four-year

3-D Printer...Motorcycle?

The 3-D printer, which can print out actual, usable objects, can create motorcycles! APWorks, part of the Airbus company, has printed a complete 3-D motorcycle body known as the Light Rider. It's more like an electric bicycle than a motorcycle. Initial aluminum frames weighed only 77 pounds (35 kilograms), which is about 30 percent lighter than a typical motorcycle frame. This printed bike can reach 50 miles (80 km) per hour and go from 0 to 30 miles (45 km) per hour in three seconds. It runs on a rechargeable battery, which can manage 35 miles (60 km) on a single charge.

group challenge is geared toward young engineers. They are tasked with making a 2016 Chevy Camaro into a fuel-efficient sports car.

Why Drive When You Can Fly?

Anyone who has ever watched the cartoon *The Jetsons* or read science fiction has probably thought about flying cars. Crowded highways and traffic jams make driving on land a real challenge in some places. So what better idea than to figure out how to fly in the air?

Engineers are hard at work on some promising airy options. Five graduates from the Massachusetts Institute of Technology (MIT)

This three-dimensional model shows the TF-X electric flying car designed by Terrafugia. It is controlled by computer for vertical takeoff and landing.

formed Terrafugia in 2006. They now have engineers, designers, certification experts, and business professionals all working for the company. In 2017, they had two possible mass-market flying cars in the works. They claim that the Transition will be a "practical" flying car that drives "at the speed of light." Two prototype models have gone on test flights. The TF-X is an electric, computer-controlled VTOL (vertical takeoff and landing) car.

In Slovakia, the AeroMobil is close to being ready to drive … or fly. The company says, "It's a real flying car, with all that a car and an aeroplane have to offer. Because of its true flexibility, you have a choice: road or air."

Others are in the works, but curiously with a lot more secrecy. California's Zee.Aero won financial support from none other than Google's cofounder Larry Page in 2016, but little information has been released. Page must be really into flying cars, though, because he also invested in Kitty Hawk. So far, Kitty Hawk has only released information on the Kitty Hawk Flyer, a car designed to fly over water. It is likely working on more, and one of the employees is Emerick Oshiro, who has experience with Google's self-driving cars. And Airbus is working on a flying car called the Vahana as well as another called the Pop.Up.

Alas, no one can rush out and buy his or her own flying car—yet. But drivers can certainly keep that idea on the back burner for a future purchase! Whether it's a flying car, a 3-D vehicle, or just lighter and safer vehicles, engineering feats will never slow down, not in the twenty-first century or beyond.

CHRONOLOGY

1769

Nicolas Cugnot develops a three-wheeled carriage.

1876

German Nikolaus Otto invents the first successful internal combustion gasoline engine.

1891

William Morrison begins producing the first electric car in the United States.

1897

Twin American brothers Francis E. and Freelan O. Stanley present the Stanley Steamer.

1900

The Elektromobil is developed and soon becomes the world's first hybrid.

1990

General Electric announces the Impact, an electric car.

2015

Tesla offers "Ludicrous Mode" in its electric cars.

2017

Audi announces the A8, which can accelerate, brake, and steer on its own.

2017

Vehicle-to-vehicle (V2V) technology in the Mercedes-Benz E-Class car allows cars to communicate with each other.

BIBLIOGRAPHY

Alliance of Automobile Manufacturers. "How Automakers Are Driving Innovation." Retrieved October 11, 2017. https://autoalliance.org/innovation.

Bogost, Ian. "When Cars Fly." *Atlantic*, May 2016. https://www.theatlantic.com/magazine/archive/2016/05/when-cars-fly/476382/.

Cox, Lauren. "Who Invented the Car? Live Science, September 12, 2017. https://www.livescience.com/37538-who-invented-the-car.html.

English, Trevor. "Will Cars of the Future Be Gyms on the Go?" Interesting Engineering, February 22, 2017. http://interestingengineering.com/cars-future-gyms-go/.

Gitlin, Jonathan. "Consulting the Engineers on What Makes the Corvette C7.R Such a Good Race Car." Ars Technica, February 9, 2017. https://arstechnica.com/cars/2017/02/consulting-the-engineers-on-what-makes-the-corvette-c7-r-such-a-good-race-car/.

Kalogianni, Alexander. "The Next 10 Years in Car Tech Will Make the Last 30 Look Like Just a Warm-up." Digital Trends, January 12, 2016. https://www.digitaltrends.com/cars/the-future-of-car-tech-a-10-year-timeline/.

Markus, Frank. "Audi Flagship Brings Long-Predicted Features to Market." Motortrend. Retrieved October 10, 2017. http://www.motortrend.com/news/2019-audi-a8-l-future-tech-features/.

McFarland, Matt. "Google's Waymo Gives Free Self-Driving Car Rides in Phoenix." CNNtech, April 25, 2017. http://money.cnn.com/2017/04/25/technology/waymo-phoenix-self-driving-cars/?iid=EL.

Mercedes Benz. "Bertha Benz: A Woman Moves the World." Retrieved October 4, 2017. https://www.mercedes-benz.com /en/mercedes-benz/classic/bertha-benz/.

Miley, Jessica. "Volvo Admits Its Self-Driving Cars Are Completely Thrown Off by Hopping Kangaroos." Interesting Engineering, July 4, 2017. http://interestingengineering.com/volvo-self -driving-cars-thrown-off-by-hopping-kangaroos/.

Petrány, Máté. "Porsche Built an Electric Cayman to Show Off 'Porsche Turbo Charging.'" *Road and Track*, October 10, 2017. http://www.roadandtrack.com/new-cars/future-cars /a12813355/porsche-built-an-electric-cayman-to-show-off -porsche-turbo-charging/.

Science Kids. "Car Facts for Kids." July 8, 2016. http://www .sciencekids.co.nz/sciencefacts/vehicles/cars.html.

US Department of Energy. "Plug-in Hybrids." Retrieved October 7, 2017. http://www.fueleconomy.gov/feg/phevtech.shtml.

GLOSSARY

autonomous Acting alone or able to act independently.

biometrics Dealing with data related to living things; also called biostatistics.

chassis The frame of an automobile or other wheeled machine.

clutch The pedal that operates a vehicle's clutch, which connects or disconnects with a car's transmission system.

commodity A raw material that can be bought and sold.

concept cars The newest cars with cutting-edge technologies.

emission A substance, like a gas, discharged into the air.

feedstock A raw material that can fuel a machine or other process.

fracking The process of injecting liquid into rock to extract gas.

ludicrous So crazy or out of line that it's funny.

piston A short cylinder fitted in a tube that moves up and down with the force of liquid or gas, such as in an internal combustion engine to create movement.

regenerative Characterized by creating something new.

semiautonomous Partly running on its own.

synthetic fuel Fuel made by chemical means.

transmission system A system in an automobile that moves power from the engine to the wheels.

FURTHER READING

Books

Harris, Tim. *Transportation Technology.* New York, NY: Cavendish Square, 2016.

Nagelhout, Ryan. *The Problem with Early Cars.* New York, NY: Gareth Stevens, 2016.

Shea, Therese. *Solving Real World Problems with Mechanical Engineering.* New York, NY: Britannica Educational Publishing, 2016.

Turner, Matt. *Genius Transportation Inventions: From the Wheel to Spacecraft.* Minneapolis, MN: Hungry Tomato, 2017.

Websites

Automobile History
www.history.com/topics/automobiles
Check out the development of cars, from Henry Ford's first model to today's cutting-edge marvels.

Automotive Engineer
www.sciencebuddies.org/science-engineering-careers/ engineering/automotive-engineer
Learn about what an auto engineer does!

History of Cars
www.dkfindout.com/uk/transport/history-cars/
Read about the development of many kinds of cars throughout history.

INDEX